This Notebook Belongs To

....

....

It's not the end

Made in the USA
Monee, IL
07 July 2026

56550090R10066